How Moon Tricked Sun

The Story of Day and Night

Janet Craig

Illustrated by
Franklin Ayres

RIGBY

2

Long, long ago there were two brothers.
The big brother was Sun.
The little brother was Moon.
They loved to run across the sky.

When Sun ran across the sky,
the Earth was warm.
When Moon ran across the sky,
the Earth was cool.
The people were very happy.

But Sun grew bigger and bigger.
After a while, he was so big that
he filled the sky.
"Make room for me!" said Moon to Sun.
"No," said Sun. "Why should I make
room for you? The people love **me**."

Sun shone and shone.
The land got hotter and hotter.
Soon the people were hot and tired.
"We miss the cool moon," they said.

Moon was small but he was clever.

"Big Brother," Moon called.

"The people do not like you any more."

"Nonsense!" said Sun. "The people love me!
They come out to see me all the time."

"Then where are they?" said Moon.

Sun looked down at the dry, hot Earth.
He saw no one.
"You see, no one loves you," said Moon.
"Go away!" said Sun.
"Make me!" said Moon.
Then, with an angry roar, Sun
chased Moon across the sky.

As Sun went down, Moon came up.
The people came out of their houses.
"At last, the cool night is here!" they said.

Sun and Moon are still
chasing each other
across the sky.
When Sun goes down
Moon comes up.
Sun brings day and
Moon brings night.